RARE

WONDROUS

THINGS

A Poetic Biography of Maria Sibylla Merian

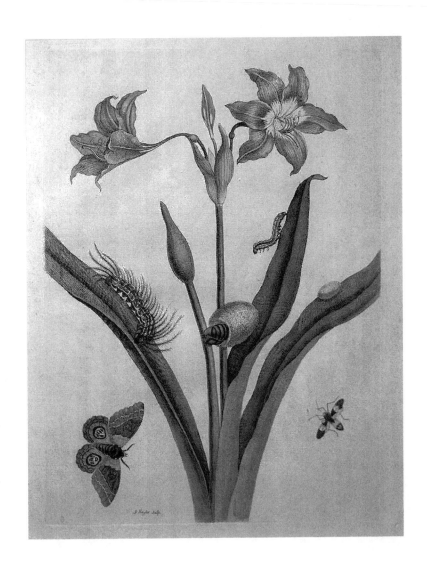

RARE
WONDROUS
THINGS

A Poetic Biography of Maria Sibylla Merian

Poems

Alyse Bensel

GREEN WRITERS PRESS | *Brattleboro, Vermont*

Printed in the United States

10 9 8 7 6 5 4 3 2 1

Green Writers Press is a Vermont-based publisher whose mission
is to spread a message of hope and renewal through the words and
images we publish. Throughout we will adhere to our commitment to
preserving and protecting the natural resources of the earth. To that
end, a percentage of our proceeds will be donated to environmental
activist groups. Green Writers Press gratefully acknowledges support
from individual donors, friends, and readers to help support the
environment and our publishing initiative.

Giving Voice to Writers & Artists Who Will Make the World a Better Place

Green Writers Press | Brattleboro, Vermont
www.greenwriterspress.com

ISBN: 978-1-7327434-0-3

COVER ARTWORK:
Maria Sibylla Merian, Plate 22, *Metamorphosis
Insectorum Surinamensium* (1705).
Used with permission from the University of
Kansas Spencer Research Library.

Quite curious, as there are many wondrous, rare things in them that have never come to light before. And no one would so easily undertake such a hard and costly journey for such things. Thus this work is not only rare now but will surely remain so.

MARIA SIBYLLA MERIAN,
letter to Johann Georg Volkammer,
OCTOBER 8, 1702

CONTENTS

RARE
WONDROUS
THINGS

A Poetic Biography of Maria Sibylla Merian

Dear Esteemed Art-Loving Reader

*Do not, dear reader, let the pleasure of your eyes be spoiled; judge
not too quickly, but read me from beginning to end.*

—Maria Sibylla Merian, Introduction
to the *Caterpillar Book*, VOLUME 2, 1783

I observe and record and obey
    those who destroy, who follow
      each tiny moon

    pinned on the underbelly
      of a tulip's praying leaf,

        signaling its slow devouring.

   Caterpillars the length
of a fingernail crack

from the egg. The chrysalis
   contains a metamorphosis
      incandescent in its hardened shell.

      Even the inchworm raises
      the length of its body
      to heaven. Caught
      in ecstasy, she praises

   what shapes
   all creatures.

Bloodless Creatures

Like the majority of living beings, this caterpillar [silkworm]
also emerges from an egg. That egg remains an egg for a year and
then, with the spring and the heat or because women warm them
for three days between their breasts, the caterpillars hatch out of
their eggs.

—Marcello Malpighi, on his findings
to the Royal Society in London, 1669

Like fine embroidery, tubes for breathing
and digestion spilled guts no naked eye
could discern. Closer. Malpighi would rent
hundreds apart to examine his eviscerated patients,
all nodding and nodding until the scalpel
split open their underbelly seams. Unrolled
translucence tied the invisible threads
that bound the moving creatures swirling
in small filigreed continents no man could
reanimate, only darken to shriveled flesh.

Apprentice, 1659

Maria's stepfather placed a vase
stuffed with chrysanthemums
and heady peonies on the table.
Flowers: A girl's first task.
She struggled to paint veined leaves,
where language failed to describe
the exact mottled design.
After the watercolors had set,
she tore off the petals, rubbing
them between her fingers.
She wished to release
decay's mortal perfume—
the bloom, the wilt.

Inheriting Theodor de Bry's Historie Americae

She's seen the idealized native, a victim
made classical myth without witness.
An homage to monsters that dwell
within monsters. The Spaniards find easy

passage by fashioning chariots from turtles
and lions. Nereids bathe close to the ship.
A soldier holds a lily in wonder, inhales
its salty fragrance. The natives must know

if these arrivals are lesser gods
who breathe water. Punishment is given
freely. No one is spared. The waves take all.
They offer gold as gifts, then pour

it molten down foreign throats. Melting flesh
muffles their screams. Columbus, alone.
John Smith, alone. These men are insistent
on the knowledge land is theirs. This primer

on violence for a girl who is shown fish fly
and the naked and clothed alike are hanged.
She mourns and delights in such wicked
perishing. Yet there is want for departure.

Ripe with Butterflies

Pregnant with her daughter
Maria's mother hung pin-struck

thoraxes and wings so their stilled
pigment could keep her company.

She scattered dried starfish
on the dresser and secreted

seashells from the curio,
sliding them between her fingers.

Maria always kept her collections free
to escape from the muslin-draped

boxes where she raised them,
plucked from the garden

like fine bits of silk. She whispered
between silence and flutter,

expecting cages but not a captor
within her bedroom walls.

Pomegranate Tree, Split Fruit and Painted Lady

Maria Sibylla Merian, c. 1665

Segmented branches lack
depth, unable to trick the eye
into believing. The disproportion
of unripe globes, the color
too thickly applied.

She layered her solution
transparent with the veins
of leaves rendered as close
to life as she could touch.
The painted lady's wings
are as thin as pressed powder
meant to cover imperfection.

Caterpillar Song

> *Just as the caterpillars transform themselves*
> *[t]hey who through their mortality*
> *again become alive*
> *just like the dead in the ground*

—Christoph Arnold, "Raupen-lied," Introduction to
Maria Sibylla Merian's *Caterpillar Book*, Volume 1, 1679

Cabbage whites yellow
like paper nearly
     preserved but fading.
     Note every stage

in copper.
Names mark decay
     sucked back to the
     roots of rosulate leaves,

bittercress collected
and placed in a dry
     cotton-lined box.

     Painters fearing mortality
     rejoice in rebirth.
One white-
mottled body molts

     five times before
     this black-tipped
butterfly can unfold.
Common insects destroy

9

and build their entire
flesh into
life sanctified
but unholy.

Overnight, their hunger
leaves nothing by morning.

Glossary for Metamorphosis I

samen, millet seed. *Caterpillar or moth eggs.*
    Does every cluster signify life? Like pills or ribbed
    pale shells or thin paper lanterns. An ant's nonpareils.
    Microscopes revealed how the heads emerge like polyps
    from their coral bud. I could tell you they are a filament
    in the crosshairs of a universe expanding. I could tell you
    what builds the earth.

ey. *Cocoon of moths or butterflies.*
    I have failed God less but you more. This is the place of
    waiting. Life hangs on thread and spit. As though the
    wind could not crush every silken covering like a tent in
    a storm.

goldlinge. *A chrysalis speckled with gold.*
    The most precious things are broken with color. I never
    wanted gold rings. Solid lasts too long, pretending to be
    forever. Not even the sun will stay. Passing comets leave
    a streak fading across the sky, promising return.

silberlinge. *A chrysalis the color of silver or mother of pearl.*
    A piece of silver clinging to a stem. You are a pendant
    burnished and kept in a silk-lined drawer, never feeling
    the hollow of my neck.

date kernel, date pit. *Butterfly or moth pupa.*
    Aristotle thought of date seeds spit to the ground.
    He never learned pupas do not arise from putrefied
    mud and shit. Every fifth-grade classroom hangs a
    mesh cage for caterpillars to change. A biology lesson.
    Transformation begins this cycle. And ends it.

After Tulipomania

The virus split the bulbs in two
   spent halves for moneylenders' fortunes.
     Greed, a waste of beauty

for beauty, crimson and white-
   struck. Where does the break,
     like a wave against a barrier,

mix disease and perfection? The silver-ground
   carpet moth keeps its diligence.
     This virus smolders away lives

when left untended. Do not burn what
   has consumed you. Pray as the moth
     bows its antennae. Keep nature

in its use, certain that God has let
   these creatures live, knowing
     each is humble, knowing we are not.

Domestic

It is odd/ when one should consider this work of mine/ as a
woman/ (who has to compile this in addition to her domestic
duties)/ as an unseemly, immoderate ambition.

Maria Sibylla Merian, Introduction
to the *Caterpillar Book*, Volume 1, 1679

Kept in jars and wooden boxes
covered with gauze, caterpillars,

beetles, silkworms can fit
through the smallest crack or die

from soaked leaves left to rot.
I've learned how to run

a house free of escaped insects
and arrange my husband's books

in the order he prefers,
place fresh irises by the east window.

Patterns mark the hours sure as a stitch.
Lessons at three. Students with

silks and paint on Tuesday,
needles and dyed linen Friday.

I note the count, double thread
to reinforce the design

just as moths surround their pupas
in silk to keep their ascendance safe.

The World Lends Its Color

I borrow sky ground
        to blue powder, Madonna-holy
and fringed iris petal.

        Each cupped rose spans
the distance traveled for miraculous color
        that imitates damp earth:

weedy woad pressed for indigo,
        green from fragrant buckthorn sap,
boiled shellfish for tyrone purple. I want

        the origins of hot springs and burning
volcanoes, molten orpiment, transcendent
        hues waiting to be rediscovered.

Visiting the Cabinets of Curiosity

> [. . . exotic insects were] shown in such a way that their origins
> and manner of reproduction were missing [. . .].

> —Maria Sibylla Merian, Preface to
> Metamorphosis Insectorum Surinamensium, 1705

Strange and stranger are the wonder
rooms that separate specimen from life.
A rattlesnake gulps her young to safety.
An opossum's grossly distorted pouch,
or a manatee's flipper, once a mermaid's
hand, have their own divided anarchy.
Spiraled narwhal horns delight
my daughters, who wish to touch
glacial waters. A vampire bat's incisors
could cut brocade. Near collapse,
these shelves are burdened by a desire
to collect but not retain knowledge.
Where I will go from here: stop
this cycle's motion, let every species
evolve into a new unified order.

Notes on What Comes from Dead Birds

. . . white worms, originating from decaying matter . . .

—Maria Sibylla Merian, Study Book

I kept the dead fieldfare
because it pulsated
from within, its small heart inflating.

I opened its plumage and skin to see
white worms in place of a heart, intestines.
I kept the bird in a wire cage,

and its body writhed
as if a hand had ripped away
its small heart. From within, an inflation

cleaved flesh from bone.
For over a fortnight
its body was eaten away.

Feathers were all that remained.
From within, its small heart inflated
and burst. The worms shriveled

and dried. I kept watch. Where has
its life gone but to
the single fly that emerged?

Glossary for Metamorphosis II

summer birds. *Butterflies.*
    Stained glass windows in flight. Their mosaics outrival
    the most intricate arrangement of stones laid for garden
    paths. They search for light, nourishing what gives
    breath.

imago. *The last stage of metamorphosis.*
    The final form before the descent into leaves or a
    piercing beaked mouth. A luscious tongue.

psyche. *Breath or soul.*
    Lungs and inhale, the air's slow hiss, escape. Aristotle
    thought of butterflies as souls balancing themselves on
    the wind in slow, uneven ascension. To breathe is to
    live, impart what we cannot use to those who need extra
    air to push forward, pull us near.

chrysalis. *Gilded.*
    The gold drops on a monarch's emerald palace
    fashioned out of crocodile skin. The most expensive
    purse.

larvae. *Mask or hobgoblin.*
    Poison pincushions set for a Mardi Gras parade,
    shedding and growing out of their own skin, drunk
    on chlorophyll. Painted cartoon eyes to fool hunters
    from above. Ridged, spiked, shiny-bumped and glossed.
    Engorged then purged to weave what could be a coffin
    or transcendence.

cocoon. *Shell.* Burlap and cotton.
    The source of silk, the stocky moth's prized procession.
    The simpler outer layer that shelters the self dissolving.

Colorfast

I once made indigo sink
into fabric and never bleed.
Crimsons and gold hues
limned brocade with a dye
that never lost sharpness.
Tulip, hyacinth, and iris
whirled across silk like a breeze
lifting up my heavy skirts,
hushing quiet and yet
bright as sin.

Housewife

I bend and rise
with the grace
of a wide-hipped
tulip. I distill
lavender, smash
cloves, repeat a kitchen
experiment to boil
dye that can bear
the cruelty of soap
and hard water.
I'm spent on the oven
coals, radiant heat.
I find myself
in throes of pin
and needle, buckled
patterns. I know soft
fabric for its
translucence. I cannot
peer through my own skin
into its veined architecture,
how my body breathes.
But a magnifying glass
will let me learn
everything concealed
within my own flesh,
trembling to erupt.

To get a moth—

Tear your hair out and wrap it in silk

Crush cloves and lavender in a marble bowl

Infuse mint tea and tar

Steep yourself in this bath

Your skin will harden

There will be no blood

Only the flimsy remains, your shoulders aching

Crack walnuts in your jaw

Only when you have been broken

Will the moth crawl out

Two Apples and Various Metamorphoses

—Maria Sibylla Merian, 1691–1699

A rustic shoulder-knot's legs curl
around just-picked apple leaves,

where its earlier tidy form
has yet to eat the upended green.

It peers to its rearing neighbor,
mottled umber moth caterpillar

reaching out for air, startled
like a white horse ready

to alight off vellum flesh.
Lined up as if on parade,

parasites invade pupa to claim
a body for another gestation.

Behind these minor forms
the sun begins rising.

Virgins in the Imperial Garden

—Maria Sibylla Merian's "company of maidens"

Her Eves before Eve practiced
on scrap. A little violet hissing
its stamen into spring air served
as their patient model. In the garden
beside the greenhouse, filled with
citrus trees and orchids from exotic
lands, their easels marked the hours.
By evening, the virgins' real work
began with long nets and careful steps.
The moths shed pollen from
their thick furred bodies. The frenetic
beating of girl heart and moth wings
in flight, one fleeing, one in pursuit,
yearning to touch something precious.

To kill a butterfly quickly

hold a darning needle
point to the flame. Let
it glow hot and red. Stick

it alive—it will die
fast with no damage
to its wings. Coat the little

cedar box where its body
is placed with lavender oil,
so worms cannot bore

in to feed. Follow these
notations here precisely.
Preserve and keep each

rare, wondrous thing
and never have it fade
if kept forever from sun

in its now still sanctuary.

Twelve Years *for* Hyles euphorbiae

[. . .] one of the longest but most pleasant transformations.

—Maria Sibylla Merian on the spurge hawk-moth

I learn patience through counting
uncertainty, record an afternoon's descent
into idleness as cells rearrange for flight,
the hawk-moth's silent ecstasy.
Every iteration has potential to stretch
and harden, reach full wingspan,
instead of lolling stunted with a body
unable to lift into late spring air. Purged
of parasites and imperfections, the pupa,
healing itself from infection, waits.
No one can guard its exterior. Ten years
I have failed. I will fail again for this beauty.

Fragments from the Caterpillar Book

> *So often has it happened that God's mysterious omnipotence*
> *and wondrous protection of such admirable lowly creatures and*
> *unworthy little birds has been welcomed and praised on high.*
> *Which has also brought me so far and finally prompted me [. . .]*
> *to present such divine wonders in a small book.*

—Maria Sibylla Merian, Introduction to the
Caterpillar Book, Volume 1, 1679

PLATE 1, Volume I, 1679. *Metamorphosis of the Silkworm with a*
White Mulberry Leaf

It's diagrammed and scattered
to fat moths expelling pale silk,
a baby's blanket deflating.

PLATE 17, Volume I, 1679. *Metamorphosis of the Lappet*

Fallen orange leaf fades to
blue. A black paisley marks
swallows in flight along its back.

PLATE 36, Volume I, 1679. *Curly Dock with Metamorphosis of the*
Small Engrailed and the Blood-Vein

Not even arterial
resting on lush clusters.
Where can they fly off
this long, heavy leaving—

PLATE 5, Volume II, 1683. *Plantain with Metamorphosis of the Bright-Line Brown-Eye*

The stout browned moth's furred neck
antennae, weedy with signifiers,
is a question mark
soon to be unraveled.

Letters to Clara in Nuremberg

Letters from Maria Sibylla Merian
to Clara Regine Scheurling, 1682–1697

My servitude is more than a matter
of business, of paint and all the things

      we both hold dear.

You have used beautiful
                  carmine for the roses.

My company of maidens praises
      your devotion to your art—

          your half-dark rose and light blue lily

give me joy greater than the riches
      of a silver cup. After

you have varnished, paint
another coat until it shines

brilliant.   I have enclosed more

    red, two shells of ground paint,

  patterns of lace
         printed on green paper (forty-two marks,
         a considerable investment).

   There are many rarities from the East and West

India—snakes brandied in jars
            sealed with wood   and stag beetles. If you
                        wish to have
    any sort of seeds or spices

    I can procure these
                    things. I take liberties for your love

of each art, the work in rendering
tulips   irises   roses

                    remaining always.

Engraved in Copper and Published Herself

My husband always stayed close
to drink, red-faced with a smile loose

like unspooled thread on the table set
aside for me as a girl, scattered

with embroidery and watercolors. I skirted
the law—my stepfather agreed to let me

watch his apprentices work coating
copper plates with wax, taking up

feathers to copy designs while they mixed
inks smelling of earth and crushed shells.

The machinery radiated elemental heat.
My mother made me scrub my ink

stained hands until they reddened raw,
palms cracked. I had the precision

of smaller hands. I accrued skill
until I could be set to marry

a man who watched my talents
grow, who needed a better family name.

He became my printing press, the source
of copper and care to wipe the ink, perfect

the line. I measured the cut into metal, a relief
bit into wax design. The ink settled into

miniature valleys made with needlepoint,
an embroidery for what lasts longer

than velvet. I washed away the excess.
I had been left so little. He gained.

Human life is like a flower

A rose dedicated to Christoph Arnold,
illustrated by Maria Sibylla Merian, April 3, 1679

A rose nearly wilted
is in its fullest bloom,
signaling the fall.

Dark Dagger

Maria Sibylla Merian, *Branch of Apricots with
a Caterpillar of the Dark Dagger*, c. 1693–1699

False eyes. Red, black,
and white fading firework
perch on a wilted teardrop leaf,
its edges chewed away.
Yellowed amber. Bruised fruit.

Has anyone so fallen
for the ripening apricot?
A small death courses up,
brilliant poison on the vine.

Manual of Piety

Everything we hear or see announces God or figures him. The song of a bird, the bleating of a lamb, the voice of a man. The sight of heaven and its stars, the air and its birds, the sea and its fish, the land and its plants and animals [. . .] Everything tells of God, everything represents him, but few ears and eyes try to hear or see him.

—Jean de Labadie, *Les Entretiens d'Espirit du Jour Chrétien, our les Réflexions Importantes du Fidèle,* 1671

Immersed so fully in greater goodness
I can hardly bear it, except to taste
bitterness, thick like wasted brocade,
without reason or love. A printing press

replicates the source of a soul
torn then healed but closed
to salvation. I am never made whole.
My lack of judgment carves

a marker for the day my acceptance
took hold. Not to say I am sinful,
but I am at least enough myself
by evening. I do not mark any pages.

Unanswered, I keep searching.

Maria at the Labadist Colony

A supplicant   a woman who
reframes her own   rebirth penitent
   and willing without need
for earthly   flesh
   she still brings each record   the notebook
to study this new country   what emerges

        from the cocoon   in her own language
ey   goldlinge   silberlinge   steeped
            in brush strokes   ordained without
those solemn vows she takes   at breakfast wearing
      roughspun clothing   breaking hard bread
   there she flickers   from verse   to what crawls
inch by inch   rooted without   the need to speak—

Walta Castle

I never read his letters. I tossed them into fire,
wasting parchment my daughters could have used

for practicing Dutch or unfamiliar tongues.
The inked words, nearly inscrutable,

flared around the edges, then up
into curling smoke that did not have enough

warmth for February's bleak days. I could have
illustrated signs for his hysteria, my conviction:

his tongue lashing out like the four-wheeled suns
of a peacock flower, brash American beauty

of destruction. Me the diligent silkworm,
spinning silently. Let this labor keep me in.

I was made for stone and mortar,
what cannot rot but be smashed into

rubble or worn down, smoothed by rain
and a winter that hides the light.

The Only Letter She Sent to Her Husband
While He Built the Wall

To think you couldn't face what bound
us. Each night you sought distance. I left
you to find yourself wrapped in a shroud,
wearing torn shoes, your heels bleeding.

You have confused your whole life with failure,
as if you could understand or soothe. I have
provided and endured, while you sink under mud
performing a better man's work until the sun boils

your hands like a sailor's, born from knotted
repetition. Try to loop the thread, soiled
as you are. I have conviction you fail
to see. These stillborn children wall me in.

Metamorphosis of the Cockchafer

Maria Sibylla Merian, Study Book

The final stage begins
with a facsimile of pain.
Dull flesh studded
with blood-red drops
turns delicate when
it hardens limb from limb,
its shell glossy chestnut,
brown and grooved
like a fine sitting
room chair. I long
to touch this crafted
thing's smooth
perfection wrought
from labor, paint,
and horsehair.

Daily Daughter

Dorothea Maria Graff

I gather caterpillars like mulberries.
I harbor their bodies in my apron pockets,

thumb the leaves where I found them.
Any moving target will do, mother says,

as it eats its way through the weeds
in the orchard or the herbs used for poultice

to ward away pain. My mother and sister resurrect
the cock-eyed look of any insect with a single

haired brush. My clumsier hands make
broader strokes, my backgrounds full

of more color than the host plant
and caterpillar's many forms. I can move

from devotee to deviant with these creatures
writhing around me, their silent hungry mouths.

Double Hyacinth, Bunch-Flowered Daffodil

Maria Sibylla Merian, Plate 2,
The New Book of Flowers, 1675–1680

The moth readies to curl
under purple fluted bells,
the remains of its former life
silhouetted against rippling petals.

Nowhere to pin lasting
perfection. Fibers brittle
with oncoming summer.
A profusion of unnamed

creatures are ready to eat
through leaves that breathe
light and drink suspended
watery atmosphere. This moth

will fly; these bulbs will shed
their blooms and begin again,
immortal in their summoning
by a retreat from the chill for heat.

Traveling Without Men on Strange Business

June 1699

The ship stopped for the right wind.
Maria walked along the Channel's cliffs
then waited below deck with paper, jars,
boxes, their cargo additional to necessary items:

a pea jacket, three pairs of stockings, four pairs
of shoes, materials for a mattress, a pickaxe,
a kettle, a pan, goods for trade. They consumed
salt pork and fish, worm-eaten biscuits,

white peas. Everything preserved.
In the slowly warming air Maria dreamed
of blue morphos in humid forests
and Amazonian women pierced with bone.

By the voyage's end, the women found
Suriname's broad shoreline, mangrove forests,
swamps, the river spilling its silt again
and again, its power beyond man's control.

A New Home in Paramaribo

People ridiculed me for seeking anything other than sugar.

—Maria Sibylla Merian

In their new home cocoons clung
to window frames, tadpoles appeared
overnight in puddles. Pearlescent lizard
eggs filled musty corners. She split
pineapples for fragrance, waiting for
those hungry creatures to begin their feast.
She cracked the door. She readied her net.

scale wing

ferrasols   highly

                weathered subsurface

low activity   clays

        in mountainous regions and   alluvial

    soils acrisols   .

              deep and dense

winged

    like the tiles of a roof   hooked or clubbed

large, shiny metallic blue

       and spectacular
perceived by eyes

    unable to focus

              visual signs

scaled

    between the molts

            the instar

Wild Wasps & Nipple Fruit

A two-woman play about Maria Sibylla Merian in
Suriname by Karen Eve Johnson

*What kind of woman is this? She is not like the other
Hollanders. No man beside her. She always has her nose in the
insects. Always why and how.*

Jacoba is a woman erased
on the ship's passenger log.
She and Maria hope to learn
of a life in heat and another life
distant and wind-struck, self-made.
A daughter is lost. A daughter is
absent offstage. Trapped inside
her own projected watercolors,
Maria flutters. Jacoba watches.

For light, Jacoba collects lantern
flies. She tells Maria how to use
bright flowers that end in death:
the moon flower, its creamy white
poison for everyone but a caterpillar.
The peacock flower, to rid oneself
of children that would wither.
She counts her life in losses,
what she cannot regain.
Maria, her mouth sharpened
by the heat, the wasps, bids her to go.
Her frustrations grow out
of fertile soil doused in sugar.

News travels slower in the heat.
The morphos daze on, oblivious.
Maria grasps onto work, yet the fever
sweats on and holds. Jacoba wonders
how one can love so many creatures
but not want to free her own.

As They Are

> *Indians, who are not well treated in their servitude of the Dutch,*
> *use [the seeds of the peacock flower] to abort their children so*
> *that they will not become slaves like them."*
>
> —Maria Sibylla Merian, *Metamorphosis*
> *Insectorum Surinamensium*, 1705

For years I fed those hungry silkworm mouths during drought.

I woke to skeletal peonies, Johanna fussing in her bassinet.

Even a namesake cannot know what is needed for both wife and husband.

My bad seeds—butterflies that will never puncture a hardened cocoon.

Or when what staggered out was barely half a living thing.

I've seen how those born starve beside their mothers.

I've seen excess and know myself lacking.

This heat shortens my breath.

Fever

I did not find in that country a suitable opportunity to carry out the insect studies I had hoped to do, as the climate there is very hot. The heat caused me great problems [. . .]

—Maria Sibylla Merian, Preface to
Metamorphosis Insectorum Surinamensium, 1705

I. [flowering above]

I long for my cocoon
gauzy and imperfect.

I'm in time to set the world in order,
specimens preserved.
All of this sugar, this waste
will bear the weight.

> *how one emerges from the other*
> *rosettes of thick, sharply toothed leaves*

Boil the sugar and let
it settle into sediment.
The riverbanks are both
sugar and silt

bodies unable to escape.
I hope these ants swarm,
consume me and everything.

> *live as a shrub rooted in the ground*
> *prone to lavishness and profusion*

46

II. [consummation]

Observe the ritual
she said, dragging a bag
of caterpillars from the palms,

> *the chances of survival*
> *blurring the contours of the body*

and watch how the day
turns to evening, despite
the rain. How you return

> *patience—a beneficial little herb*
> *a large sugar jar*
> *ordering her life histories*

despite these porous walls
open to perpetual renewal,

wood and plant rot
ripped away.

There she watches
those who would not touch

the beautiful hairs
ticked with beady poison,
enflaming flesh.

No god can have
dominion over this.

III. [pain]

Numbed, cured by it,

without the knowledge of synapses
or the hesitation before reaching
out to grab a flower made of wasps

curled like yellow petals
as if in sleep or just waiting
to pierce and protect.

Is pain the reaction
or the reaction to the reaction?
A chemical coursing
through shorted nerves

> *greatly enlarged, boat-like and brightly colored*
> *with bodies parallel and touching*

and stunted or growing
from this sharpness.

IV. [surpass]

In standing her body takes the weight
of the fall and conceives

a thousand tiny caterpillars.
And she has split

and consumes all of the air
around her, striving to become

this incessant need
to live in this caterpillar body,

seething and pushing out from her skin.

Bursting at the seams
she lets the caterpillars roll her

>   *weakly fluttering, delicate*
>   *in concrete fragments*

to the leafy outside, and the hammock
and wood walls and gauze

remain barren, inhospitable to this life.

V. [bed]

I want a girdle to attach to the leaf
I do not want to fall without cushioning

    small or absent

My body, all minerals, can break
There is no more transformation

    a puzzling genus

I want to move between the instars
I want to spin myself up and take flight

Most Infamous

Cockroaches [. . .] manage to get into chests and cupboards through the joints and keyholes, where they then spoil everything . . .

—Maria Sibylla Merian, *Metamorphosis Insectorum Surinamensium*, 1705

Cockroaches shine into the infinite
exotic grotesque, infesting bedclothes
and sugar. Suriname's jungles housed
insect cities that multiplied into elisions
sliding around dark corners, poised
at the edges.
              In Bermuda I walked on
ground shuddering with what I knew
would out-survive every black witch moth.
If only I could have anticipated sudden
movement from above—that raised hand
ready to obliterate on a sedentary whim.

Anansi the Spider Devours the Hummingbird

> *When they fail to find ants they take small birds from their nests*
> *and suck all the blood from their bodies.*

> —Maria Sibylla Merian, Plate 18, *Guava tree with army*
> *ants, pink-toed tarantulas, and ruby topaz hummingbird,*
> *Metamorphosis Insectorum Surinamensium,* 1705

The spirits have begun to consume smaller
suckling forms, those hummingbird wings
buzzing beside her ear. What a racket.
Maria never witnessed the act, just what was
whispered to her after she stopped
at the rainforest's edge to find that bird,
smaller than a peach, with its throat torn out.
I've seen how they go for the arteries,
Maria—even praying mantises will grip
a sphinx moth, its wings humming
so loud I thought a bird was trapped
in heavy grass. That perfect sphere
between prey and predator is too incredible.
Maria, you needed to horrify those
armchair naturalists. You gave them
something good to talk about, the only act
of aggression those men could seek to disprove.

Witchcraft and A Woman's Worth

Dürer's snails and armored rhinoceros
        roamed the town of Darien. The rain poured
                thousands of tiny green frogs

mouths agape for worms unwilling
        to drown. Boguet wished away
                New World's sin with its witches

buried in the soil, ready to rebuild again.
        She imagined the secrets
                bound to keep for providence

shining brilliance alone,
        ascension inherent in her soul
                or a sign of witchcraft. If she followed

the heavenly signs, her hands
        caked with dirt, she could keep all this filth
                and uncleanly duty hidden in her pockets.

Kerkestraat

> [. . .] *the costs involved in carrying out such a project made me*
> *hesitant at first; but finally I resolved to do it.*
>
> Maria Sibylla Merian, Preface to *Metamorphosis*
> *Insectorum Surinamensium*, 1705

Craving light, moths
beat their wings beside
my ears. I suspend desire.
The rain leaves the streets
without any recollection
of rain. The morning
street traffic fills my head
with a noise that shuddered
through the night. I rearrange
these fragments into a legacy,
where I can breathe life
into so many blank pages.

Classification

—Georgius Everhardus Rumphius,
D'Amboinsche Rariteikamer, 1705

I illustrated the shells as he wished—placed in a perfect line,
by genus, species. His new order. The common names pasted
over to avoid confusion. Each shell perfect, small, unassuming
in the way they pointed toward some still fleeting progression,
a melody not quite on the tip of my tongue.

Illustration as Memento Mori

I catalogue near-death beauty
on needled veins, the slow
flexing wings made for midday
basking. Little token near-gone,
you are all color, no weight,
buoyant and alone. I have
searched like that, aimless,
circling for the right angle,
the best nectar. It can be
my poison, too. That drop
from the Lethe—sleep.
Will you be living or dead
when the ink has dried?
Will you even be seen at all?

Without Document

Out of the Chrysalis: A Portrait of Maria Sibylla Merian, 2008

I find a little icon
of an image left
in online stasis. I search
with *no results found.*
A preview night at Stanford,
Penn, where someone
might have understood.

The ending in trashed footage,
wiped hard drives, notes
tossed in bins: plans on
indefinite hold.

I *click* and *click* and *click.*
The URL is broken.
I reread the abandoned pages.
Maria, you are still in pieces.

First and Final Portrait

George Gsell, c. 1700

If I reach toward your careworn face,
fortunes exhausted on Suriname, will I know the cost?

What if I told you the Germans made you
glamorous, rose-tinted and coiffed

with an upturned smile, for the mark.
You are stoic in old age. The fever

has bound you to a chair. You stiffen
your back for the sake of etiquette.

The scarlet ibis merely recedes.
A common moth dives behind the drapery.

In your overstuffed study, you gesture
to somewhere else, to anywhere but there.

Women of Art and Science
at the Rembrandt House Museum

Amsterdam, March 2008

Small placards direct me to observe

egg, pupa, and butterfly arranged
around host plant. Her daughters
could not quite imitate the movement—

she never relied on pinned thoraxes that brittle
when stored in glass cases. Only what moves,
what can escape.
                I am afraid of changing
how dust measures a corner. Even still

resurrection occurs without record.

21st Century Domestic

Radish leaves soaked under the faucet
sprout squirming children that grow
into sphinx moths or yellow paper
whites littering the kitchen floor.

She must tiptoe around their sleeping
bodies and feed them drops of sugar water
off her index finger. The click of the oven
sends them into a fury, so she adapts

a raw diet, eats only kale, leaves
out her oldest books for them to feast
on, until the day she opens the closet
to find the wedding dress eaten whole:

the moths drunk with silk, satiated
and ready to depart these crumbling walls.

Merian's Brush

A moth nicknamed after Maria Sibylla Merian

Plum-blue beating heart hanging off thin stalk.

She peeled back the spun cocoon, pupating coils swaddled
amidst filmy strands.

If a moth were a crystal, it would beat within its diamond-
studded span.

Harsher still, it molts off the red waving banner unfurling
behind itself.

The pale tussock incarnates to dew drops, silk scarf, yellowed
jester, dyed cotton wings.

Plucked together on a straightened tree branch, a hushed
moving vibrant—

Saturated horsehair leaves no finer trace.

As a Young Boy, Nabokov Studies Maria's Butterflies

Caught in thrall by this final imago,
he's fascinated by so frail a thing
resilient in its lithe black body,
blue iridescent wings, and unblinking
eyes splayed in watercolor, compressed
into the pinned boards of duller minds
who have forgotten how to imagine
the dead. He reanimates the exotic
knowing these lesser gods of death,
their dominion some far-off jungle,
traverse the equator daily, sent off
into the hot air he yearns for.
On the folio's pages he imparts
palmed heat, looking to the latitudes.

Biographical Subject

If what I love is ungraspable,
like a cat-eyed marble that
easily slips out of my hands,
how much netting will it take
for me to cocoon its brilliance?

I yearn for greener places closer
to the ocean, clear rivers reflecting
the colors of a thousand insects.
I memorize their jeweled names.
I look up flight costs, luxury hotels,
count down the hours to departure.

The thoroughfares have been mapped.
I can't bear to shut myself out.

Acknowledgements

I would like to extend my thanks to the editors of the following journals, in which versions of these poems first appeared:

Blue Earth Review: "Domestic," "Women of Art and Science at the Rembrandt House Museum"
Bone Bouquet: "[pain]"
burntdistrict: "[flowering above]"
The Fourth River: "What Comes from Dead Birds"
Heron Tree: "21st Century Domestic"
Isthmus: "Letters to Clara In Nürnberg," "Pomegranate Tree, Split Fruit and Painted Lady"
IthacaLit: "Maria at the Labadist Colony," "The Only Letter She Sent to Her Husband While He Built the Wall"
Menacing Hedge: "As They Are," "Colorfast," "Witchcraft and A Woman's Worth"
Mid-American Review: "Glossary for Metamorphosis I"
Rogue Agent: "Housewife"
Ruminate Magazine: "After Tulipomania," "Caterpillar Poem"
Sugared Water: "Illustration as Memento Mori"
Sugar Mule: "Merian's Brush," "scale wing," "To get a moth—"
Spiral Orb: "Dear Esteemed Art-Loving Reader"
Zone 3: "Anansi the Spider Devours the Hummingbird," "Daily Daughter"

I am forever thankful to Caroline Shea, Dede Cummings, and all of the editors at Green Writers Press for believing in my work and giving this book a loving home.

My gratitude to the exhibition "Maria Sibylla Merian & Daughters: Women of Art and Science," a project between the Museum Het Rembrandthuis and J. Paul Getty Museum, which sparked my interest in Maria Sibylla Merian and her daughters while I was visiting Amsterdam in March 2008.

I am grateful to the Hall Center for the Humanities and the English Department at the University of Kansas for their generous support of my work.

This collection would not exist without the support and encouragement from so many people at the University of Kansas and beyond, including my dear mentor and friend Megan Kaminski, Laura Moriarty, Ann Rowland, Lee Ann Roripaugh, Patrizio Ceccagnoli, Misty Schieberle, Geraldo Sousa, and visiting scholar N. Katherine Hayles. In Lawrence, Kris Coffey, Lesley Ann Wheeler, Danny Caine, and Amanda Hemmingsen. Always, Adam Mills. In State College, Camille Yvette-Welsch. And on an island in the Caribbean, José.

Notes

The epigraph that precedes this collection is from the monograph *Maria Sibylla Merian: Artist and Naturalist*, edited by Kurt Wettengl (1998). The appendix includes a series of Merian's letters, many of which were originally translated and published by Elisabeth Rücker.

"Dear Esteemed, Art-Loving Reader": The epigraph is from the monograph *Maria Sibylla Merian: Artist and Naturalist*, edited by Kurt Wettengl.

"Bloodless Creatures": The epigraph is quoted from Ella Reitsma's *Maria Sibylla Merian & Daughters: Women of Art and Science*, p. 68.

"Inheriting Theodor de Bry's *Historie Americae*": Johann Theodor de Bry (1528–1598), a prominent engraver and publisher, was Merian's step-grandfather. He is best known for his engravings of the Americas, which were based on explorers' descriptions, as he never traveled to the Americas himself.

"*Pomegranate Tree, Split Fruit and Painted Lady, 1665*": Art historians consider this watercolor-on-vellum as Merian's first completed painting, but altogether lacking in the skill she would later acquire.

"Glossary for Metamorphosis I": Further explanation of Merian's terms can be found in Ella Reitsma's *Maria Sibylla Merian & Daughters: Women of Art and Science*, pp. 72–75.

"After Tulipomania": Tulipomania reached its peak in the Netherlands in the 1630s. Merian references the tulip craze in her introduction to the *Caterpillar Book* as a reminder of the greed that occurred during that period.

"Maria's Notes on What Comes from Dead Birds": "One day [Merian] was given a dead fieldfare. Although the creature was dead, its body was moving up and down. Naturalist Merian was curious to know how this could be. She opened its plumage and skin and was astonished to see lots of 'white worms' inside the bird. She transferred the squirming mas to a small cage and observed how the maggot-laden body was eaten away during a fortnight. Finally, she counted '156 eggs' [pupae], form which only one fly emerged, the rest dried out" (Katharina Schmidt-Loske, "Historical sketch: Maria Sibylla Merian—Metamorphosis of Insects," p. 8).

Two Apples and Various Metamorphoses: The epigraph is from Ella Reitsma's *Maria Sibylla Merian & Daughters: Women of Art and Science*, p. 123.

"Twelve Years for *Hyles euphorbia*": The epigraph is from Katharina Schmidt-Loske's "Historical sketch: Maria Sibylla Merian—Metamorphosis of Insects," p. 7.

"Fragments from the *Caterpillar Book*," "*Manual of Piety*," "Visiting the Cabinets of Curiosity," and "Kerkestraat" all use epigraphs of translations of Merian cited in Kurt Wettengl's "Maria Sibylla Merian Artist and Naturalist Between Frankfurt and Suriname," from *Maria Sibylla Merian: Artist and Naturalist* (1998).

"Letters to Clara in Nürnberg": Some of the lines in this poem have been adopted from Merian's correspondence with Clara Regine Scheurling. The letters can be found in Kurt Wettengl's *Maria Sibylla Merian: Artist and Naturalist* (1998).

"Human life is like a flower": The title is from a translation of Merian cited in Werner Taegert's "'Human Life Is Like A Flower.' Maria Sibylla Merian's Stammuch Water-Colours," from *Maria Sibylla Merian: Artist and Naturalist* (1998). This phrase has also been translated as "Every man is like a flower" in Ella Reitsma's *Maria Sibylla Merian & Daughters: Women of Art and Science*, p. 66.

"Manual of Piety": The *Manual of Piety* was a text used by the Labadists, an extreme Protestant sect started by Jean de Labadie and continued by his sisters. The Labadists were a central colonizing force in Suriname.

"The Only Letter She Sent to Her Husband While He Built the Wall": The epigraph is from Ella Reitsma's *Maria Sibylla Merian & Daughters: Women of Art and Science*, p. 92. Reitsma quotes from Petrus Dittelbach's *The Decline and Fall of the Labadists*.

"A New Home in Paramaribo": The epigraph is from Natalie Zemon Davis' *Women on the Margins*, p. 173.

"As They Are": The epigraph is from Natalie Zemon Davis' *Women on the Margins*, pp. 185–186.

"Fever": Parts of this sequence were created using a cut-up method of lines from guidebooks to Suriname, Maria's own writings, Aphra Behn's *Oroonoko* (1668), and historians' commentary on Maria's work.

"Most Infamous": The epigraph is from Ella Reitsma's *Maria Sibylla Merian & Daughters: Women of Art and Science*, p. 189.

"Anansi the Spider Devours the Hummingbird": The most infamous plate from the *Suriname Book*, Plate 18 illustrates a tarantula eating a hummingbird. The epigraph is from Natalie Zemon Davis' *Women on the Margins*, p. 183.

"Merian's Brush": In addition to this *Lepidoptera* species, eight butterflies, two beetles, nine plant species, and counting, have been named after Merian.

"First and Final Portrait": George Gsell (1673–1740) was Dorothea Maria's husband and a Swiss painter.

"As a Young Boy, Nabokov Studies Maria's Butterflies": Vladimir Nabokov noted that Merian's watercolors first inspired his interest in butterflies and entomology.

Selected Bibliography

Significant historical and biographical work has been undertaken on Maria Sibylla Merian's illustrations and life story. I am indebted to the prose biographies, monographs, and facsimiles that have been readily available during my research. The following texts were especially helpful for me during this project.

Davis, Natalie Zemon. *Women on the Margins: Three Seventeenth-Century Lives*. Cambridge, MA: Harvard University Press, 1995.

Holland, Eckhard, Ed. *Maria Sibylla Merian: The St. Petersburg Watercolors*. New York: Prestel, 2003.

Reitsma, Ella. *Maria Sibylla Merian & Daughters: Women of Art and Science*. Zwolle: Waanders Publishers, 2008.

Todd, Kim. *Chrysalis: Maria Sibylla Merian and the Secrets of Metamorphosis*. New York: Harcourt, 2007.

Wettengl, Kurt, Ed. *Maria Sibylla Merian: Artist and Naturalist*. Verlag Gerd Hatje, 1998.

Zapperi, Giovanna. "Woman's Reappearance: Rethinking the Archive in Contemporary Art—Feminist Perspectives." *Feminist Review* 105 (2013): 21-47.